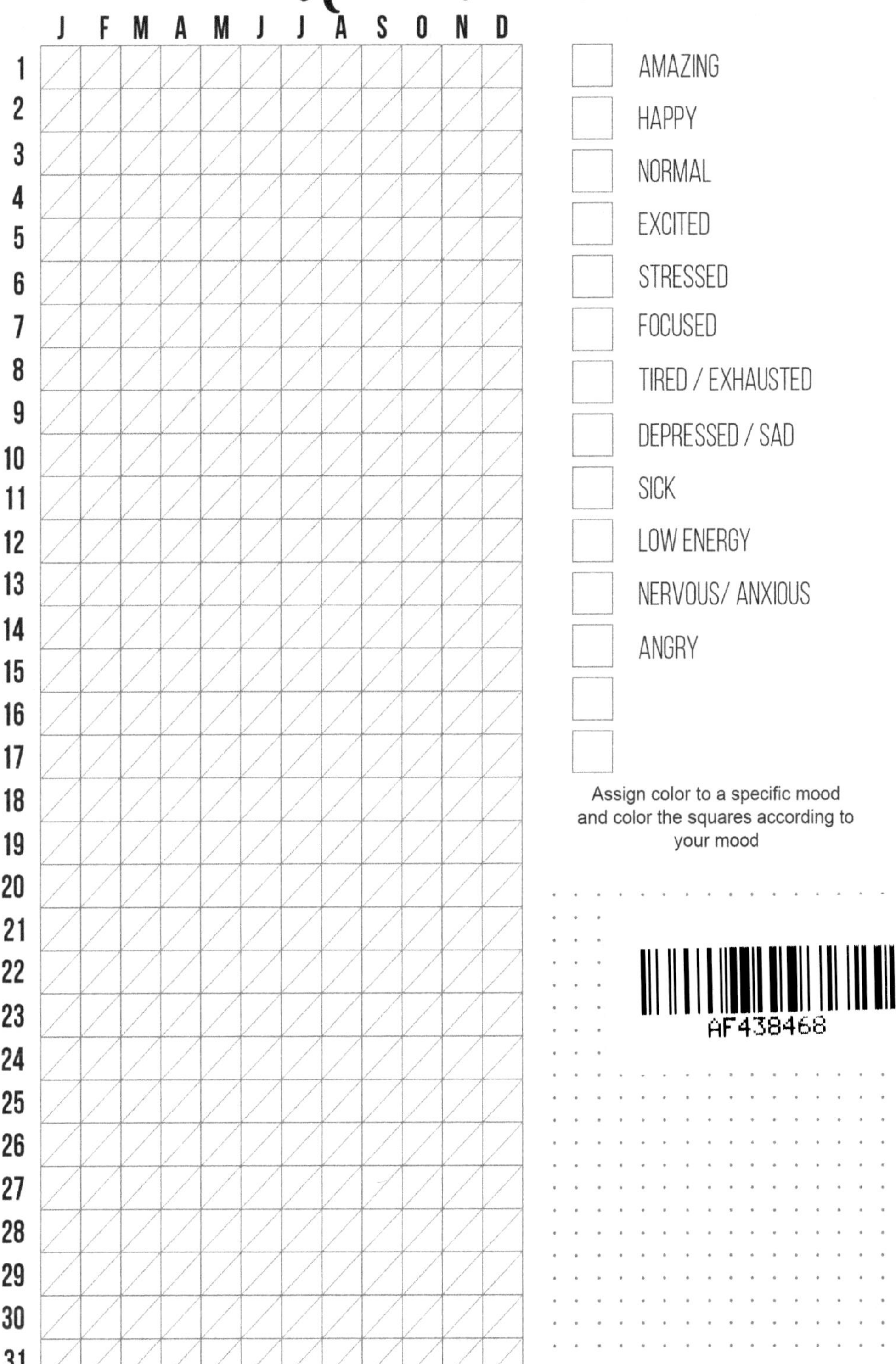

Mood Tracker
J F M A M J J A S O N D
1
2
3
4
5
6
7
8
9
10
11
12
13
14
15
16
17
18
19
20
21
22
23
24
25
26
27
28
29
30
31
AMAZING
HAPPY
NORMAL
EXCITED
STRESSED
FOCUSED
TIRED / EXHAUSTED
DEPRESSED / SAD
SICK
LOW ENERGY
NERVOUS/ ANXIOUS
ANGRY
Assign color to a specific mood
and color the squares according to
your mood
AF438468

Mood Tracker

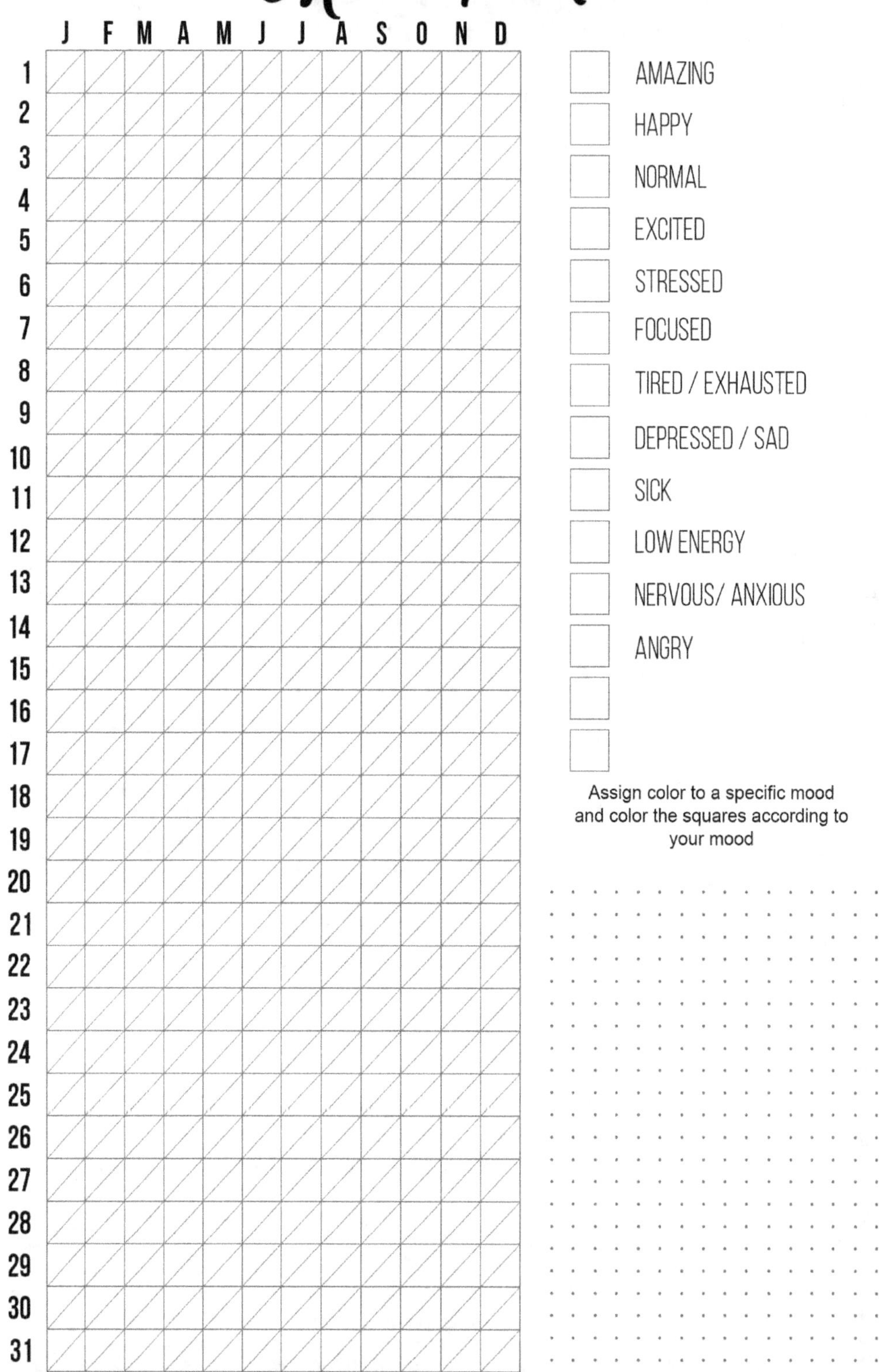

Mood Tracker

J F M A M J J A S O N D

☐	AMAZING
☐	HAPPY
☐	NORMAL
☐	EXCITED
☐	STRESSED
☐	FOCUSED
☐	TIRED / EXHAUSTED
☐	DEPRESSED / SAD
☐	SICK
☐	LOW ENERGY
☐	NERVOUS/ ANXIOUS
☐	ANGRY
☐	
☐	

Assign color to a specific mood
and color the squares according to
your mood

Mood Tracker

J F M A M J J A S O N D

	AMAZING
	HAPPY
	NORMAL
	EXCITED
	STRESSED
	FOCUSED
	TIRED / EXHAUSTED
	DEPRESSED / SAD
	SICK
	LOW ENERGY
	NERVOUS/ ANXIOUS
	ANGRY

Assign color to a specific mood
and color the squares according to
your mood

Mood Tracker

J F M A M J J A S O N D

1
2
3
4
5
6
7
8
9
10
11
12
13
14
15
16
17
18
19
20
21
22
23
24
25
26
27
28
29
30
31

AMAZING

HAPPY

NORMAL

EXCITED

STRESSED

FOCUSED

TIRED / EXHAUSTED

DEPRESSED / SAD

SICK

LOW ENERGY

NERVOUS/ ANXIOUS

ANGRY

Assign color to a specific mood
and color the squares according to
your mood

Mood Tracker

J F M A M J J A S O N D

1
2
3
4
5
6
7
8
9
10
11
12
13
14
15
16
17
18
19
20
21
22
23
24
25
26
27
28
29
30
31

- [ ] AMAZING
- [ ] HAPPY
- [ ] NORMAL
- [ ] EXCITED
- [ ] STRESSED
- [ ] FOCUSED
- [ ] TIRED / EXHAUSTED
- [ ] DEPRESSED / SAD
- [ ] SICK
- [ ] LOW ENERGY
- [ ] NERVOUS/ ANXIOUS
- [ ] ANGRY
- [ ]
- [ ]

Assign color to a specific mood and color the squares according to your mood

Mood Tracker

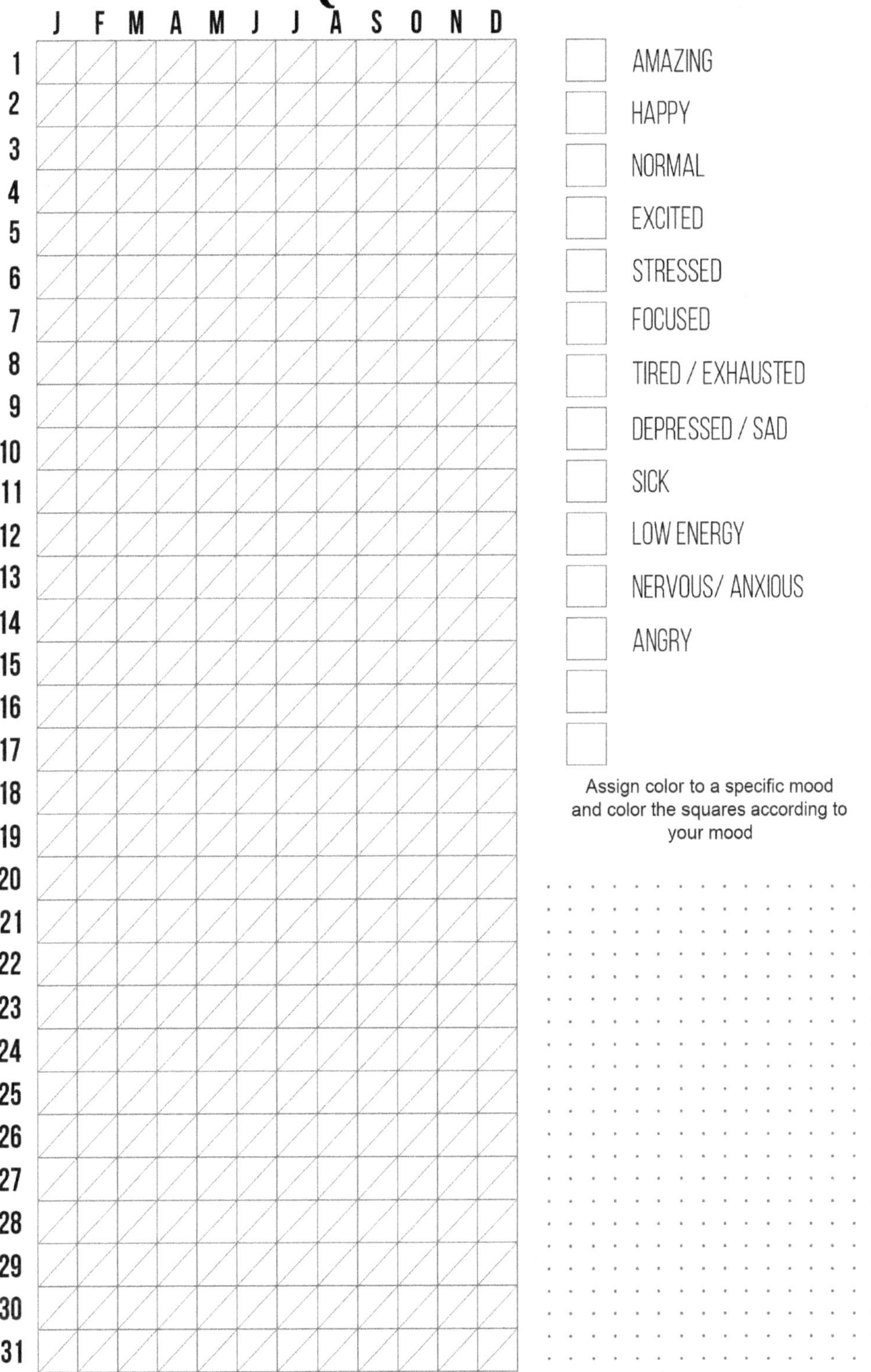

Mood Tracker

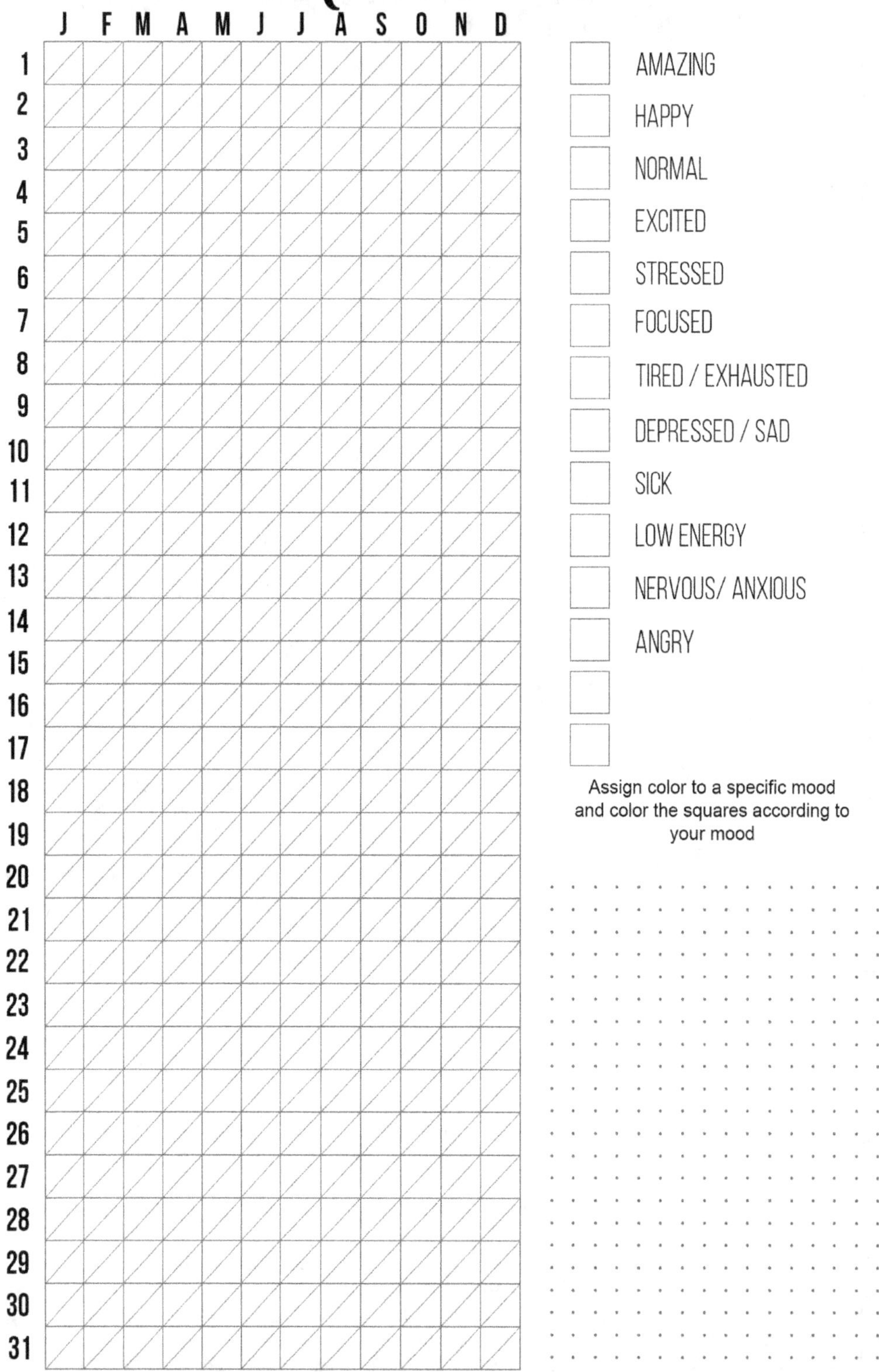

Mood Tracker

J F M A M J J A S O N D

1 2 3 4 5 6 7 8 9 10 11 12 13 14 15 16 17 18 19 20 21 22 23 24 25 26 27 28 29 30 31

- [ ] AMAZING
- [ ] HAPPY
- [ ] NORMAL
- [ ] EXCITED
- [ ] STRESSED
- [ ] FOCUSED
- [ ] TIRED / EXHAUSTED
- [ ] DEPRESSED / SAD
- [ ] SICK
- [ ] LOW ENERGY
- [ ] NERVOUS/ ANXIOUS
- [ ] ANGRY
- [ ]
- [ ]

Assign color to a specific mood
and color the squares according to
your mood

Mood Tracker

J F M A M J J A S O N D

| | 1 | 2 | 3 | 4 | 5 | 6 | 7 | 8 | 9 | 10 | 11 | 12 | 13 | 14 | 15 | 16 | 17 | 18 | 19 | 20 | 21 | 22 | 23 | 24 | 25 | 26 | 27 | 28 | 29 | 30 | 31 |

AMAZING

HAPPY

NORMAL

EXCITED

STRESSED

FOCUSED

TIRED / EXHAUSTED

DEPRESSED / SAD

SICK

LOW ENERGY

NERVOUS/ ANXIOUS

ANGRY

Assign color to a specific mood and color the squares according to your mood

Mood Tracker

J F M A M J J A S O N D

1
2
3
4
5
6
7
8
9
10
11
12
13
14
15
16
17
18
19
20
21
22
23
24
25
26
27
28
29
30
31

AMAZING

HAPPY

NORMAL

EXCITED

STRESSED

FOCUSED

TIRED / EXHAUSTED

DEPRESSED / SAD

SICK

LOW ENERGY

NERVOUS/ ANXIOUS

ANGRY

Assign color to a specific mood
and color the squares according to
your mood

Mood Tracker

J F M A M J J A S O N D

	AMAZING
	HAPPY
	NORMAL
	EXCITED
	STRESSED
	FOCUSED
	TIRED / EXHAUSTED
	DEPRESSED / SAD
	SICK
	LOW ENERGY
	NERVOUS/ ANXIOUS
	ANGRY

Assign color to a specific mood
and color the squares according to
your mood

Mood Tracker

	J	F	M	A	M	J	J	A	S	O	N	D

J F M A M J J A S O N D

1
2
3
4
5
6
7
8
9
10
11
12
13
14
15
16
17
18
19
20
21
22
23
24
25
26
27
28
29
30
31

- AMAZING
- HAPPY
- NORMAL
- EXCITED
- STRESSED
- FOCUSED
- TIRED / EXHAUSTED
- DEPRESSED / SAD
- SICK
- LOW ENERGY
- NERVOUS/ ANXIOUS
- ANGRY

Assign color to a specific mood
and color the squares according to
your mood

Mood Tracker

Mood Tracker

J F M A M J J A S O N D

1
2
3
4
5
6
7
8
9
10
11
12
13
14
15
16
17
18
19
20
21
22
23
24
25
26
27
28
29
30
31

- AMAZING
- HAPPY
- NORMAL
- EXCITED
- STRESSED
- FOCUSED
- TIRED / EXHAUSTED
- DEPRESSED / SAD
- SICK
- LOW ENERGY
- NERVOUS/ ANXIOUS
- ANGRY

Assign color to a specific mood
and color the squares according to
your mood

Mood Tracker

J F M A M J J A S O N D

1
2
3
4
5
6
7
8
9
10
11
12
13
14
15
16
17
18
19
20
21
22
23
24
25
26
27
28
29
30
31

AMAZING

HAPPY

NORMAL

EXCITED

STRESSED

FOCUSED

TIRED / EXHAUSTED

DEPRESSED / SAD

SICK

LOW ENERGY

NERVOUS/ ANXIOUS

ANGRY

Assign color to a specific mood
and color the squares according to
your mood

Mood Tracker

Mood Tracker

Mood Tracker

	J	F	M	A	M	J	J	A	S	O	N	D
1												
2												
3												
4												
5												
6												
7												
8												
9												
10												
11												
12												
13												
14												
15												
16												
17												
18												
19												
20												
21												
22												
23												
24												
25												
26												
27												
28												
29												
30												
31												

- ☐ AMAZING
- ☐ HAPPY
- ☐ NORMAL
- ☐ EXCITED
- ☐ STRESSED
- ☐ FOCUSED
- ☐ TIRED / EXHAUSTED
- ☐ DEPRESSED / SAD
- ☐ SICK
- ☐ LOW ENERGY
- ☐ NERVOUS / ANXIOUS
- ☐ ANGRY
- ☐
- ☐

Assign color to a specific mood and color the squares according to your mood

Mood Tracker

J F M A M J J A S O N D

☐	AMAZING
☐	HAPPY
☐	NORMAL
☐	EXCITED
☐	STRESSED
☐	FOCUSED
☐	TIRED / EXHAUSTED
☐	DEPRESSED / SAD
☐	SICK
☐	LOW ENERGY
☐	NERVOUS/ ANXIOUS
☐	ANGRY
☐	
☐	

Assign color to a specific mood
and color the squares according to
your mood

Mood Tracker

J F M A M J J A S O N D

	AMAZING
	HAPPY
	NORMAL
	EXCITED
	STRESSED
	FOCUSED
	TIRED / EXHAUSTED
	DEPRESSED / SAD
	SICK
	LOW ENERGY
	NERVOUS/ ANXIOUS
	ANGRY

Assign color to a specific mood and color the squares according to your mood

Mood Tracker

J F M A M J J A S O N D

1
2
3
4
5
6
7
8
9
10
11
12
13
14
15
16
17
18
19
20
21
22
23
24
25
26
27
28
29
30
31

AMAZING

HAPPY

NORMAL

EXCITED

STRESSED

FOCUSED

TIRED / EXHAUSTED

DEPRESSED / SAD

SICK

LOW ENERGY

NERVOUS/ ANXIOUS

ANGRY

Assign color to a specific mood
and color the squares according to
your mood

Mood Tracker

	J	F	M	A	M	J	J	A	S	O	N	D
1												
2												
3												
4												
5												
6												
7												
8												
9												
10												
11												
12												
13												
14												
15												
16												
17												
18												
19												
20												
21												
22												
23												
24												
25												
26												
27												
28												
29												
30												
31												

- [ ] AMAZING
- [ ] HAPPY
- [ ] NORMAL
- [ ] EXCITED
- [ ] STRESSED
- [ ] FOCUSED
- [ ] TIRED / EXHAUSTED
- [ ] DEPRESSED / SAD
- [ ] SICK
- [ ] LOW ENERGY
- [ ] NERVOUS/ ANXIOUS
- [ ] ANGRY
- [ ]
- [ ]

Assign color to a specific mood
and color the squares according to
your mood

Mood Tracker

J F M A M J J A S O N D

1
2
3
4
5
6
7
8
9
10
11
12
13
14
15
16
17
18
19
20
21
22
23
24
25
26
27
28
29
30
31

AMAZING

HAPPY

NORMAL

EXCITED

STRESSED

FOCUSED

TIRED / EXHAUSTED

DEPRESSED / SAD

SICK

LOW ENERGY

NERVOUS / ANXIOUS

ANGRY

Assign color to a specific mood
and color the squares according to
your mood

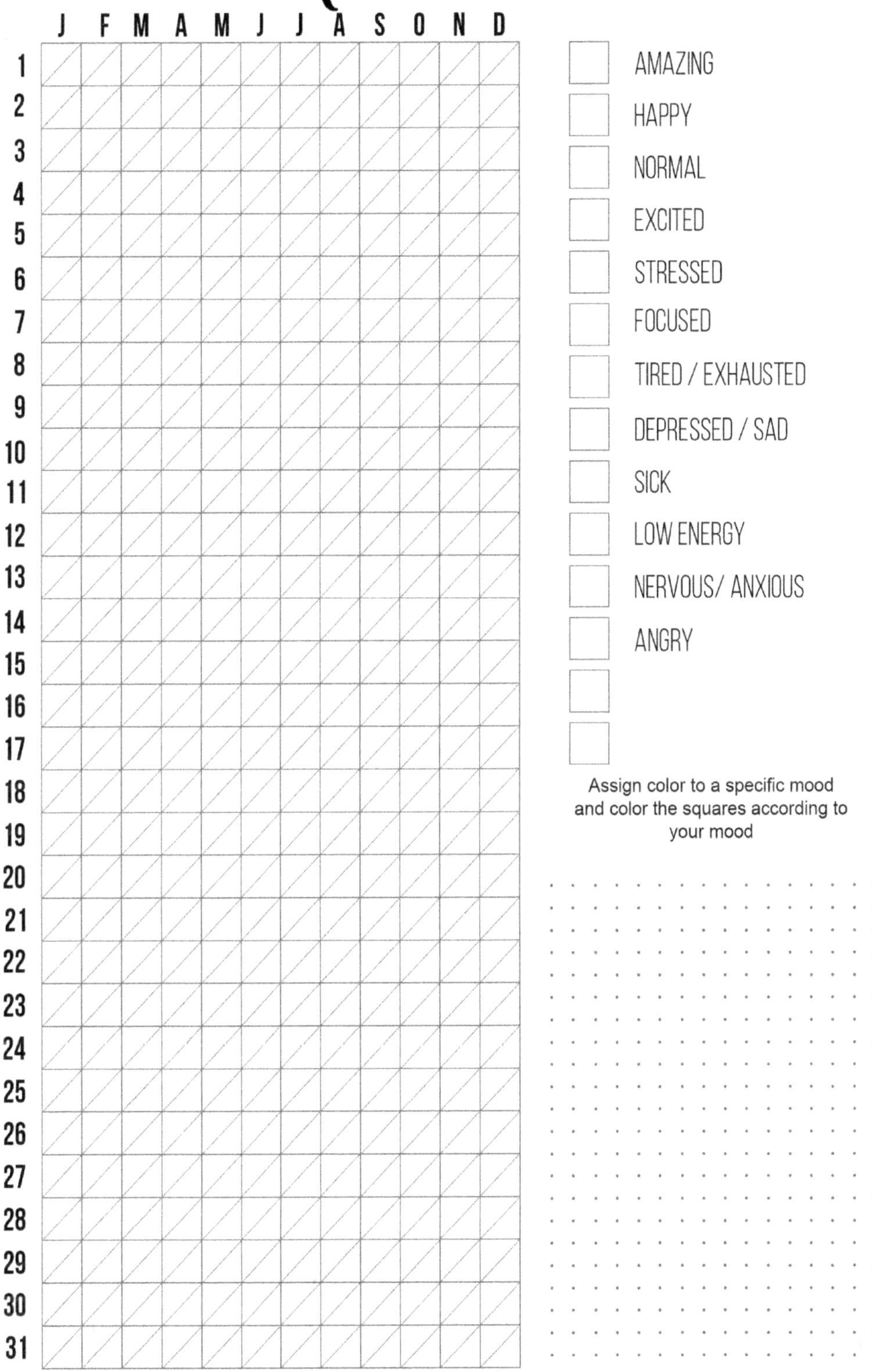

Mood Tracker

J F M A M J J A S O N D

1
2
3
4
5
6
7
8
9
10
11
12
13
14
15
16
17
18
19
20
21
22
23
24
25
26
27
28
29
30
31

AMAZING
HAPPY
NORMAL
EXCITED
STRESSED
FOCUSED
TIRED / EXHAUSTED
DEPRESSED / SAD
SICK
LOW ENERGY
NERVOUS/ ANXIOUS
ANGRY

Assign color to a specific mood
and color the squares according to
your mood

Mood Tracker

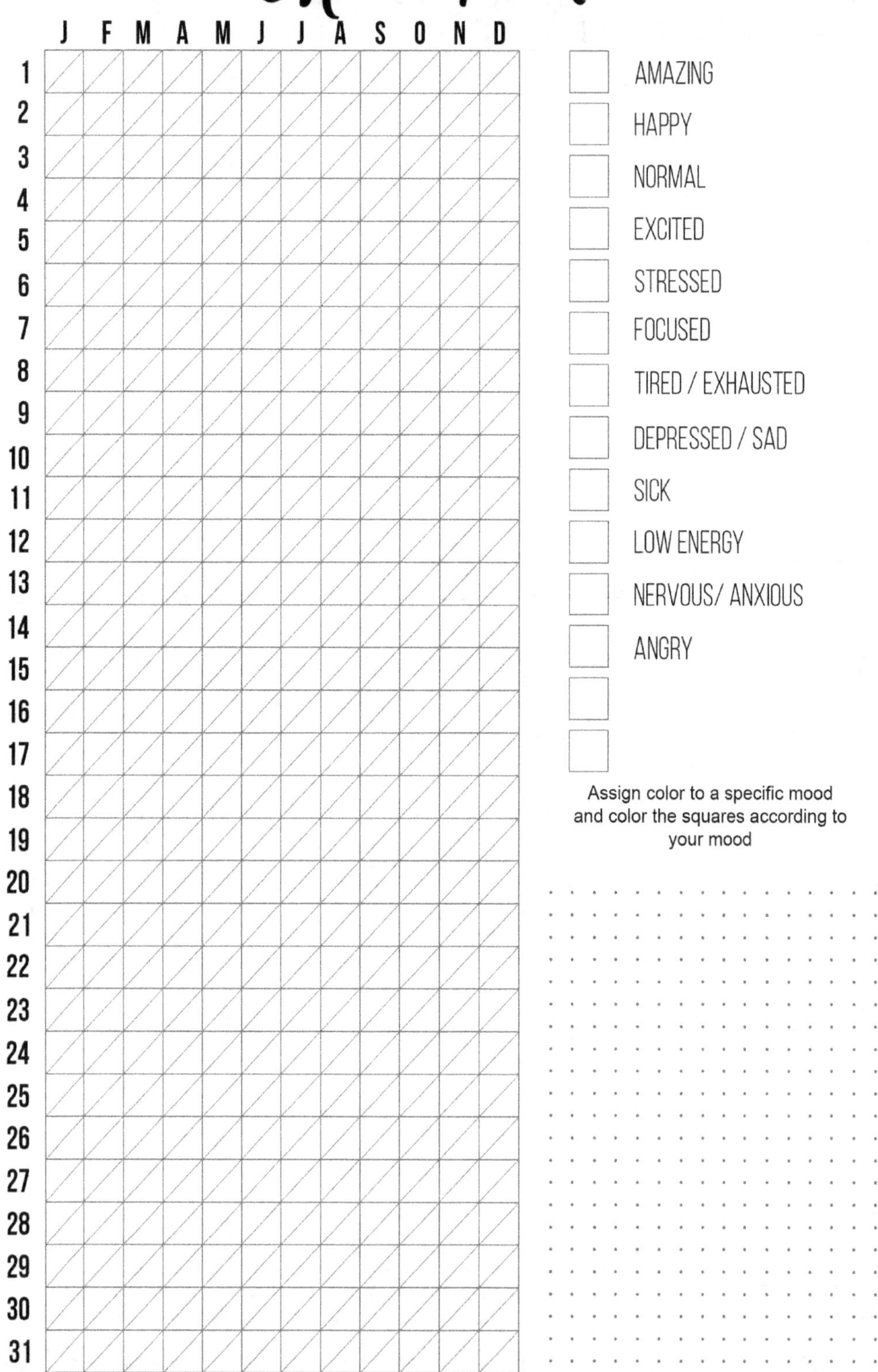

Mood Tracker

J F M A M J J A S O N D

AMAZING

HAPPY

NORMAL

EXCITED

STRESSED

FOCUSED

TIRED / EXHAUSTED

DEPRESSED / SAD

SICK

LOW ENERGY

NERVOUS/ ANXIOUS

ANGRY

Assign color to a specific mood
and color the squares according to
your mood

Mood Tracker

J F M A M J J A S O N D

1
2
3
4
5
6
7
8
9
10
11
12
13
14
15
16
17
18
19
20
21
22
23
24
25
26
27
28
29
30
31

- AMAZING
- HAPPY
- NORMAL
- EXCITED
- STRESSED
- FOCUSED
- TIRED / EXHAUSTED
- DEPRESSED / SAD
- SICK
- LOW ENERGY
- NERVOUS/ ANXIOUS
- ANGRY

Assign color to a specific mood and color the squares according to your mood

Mood Tracker

	J	F	M	A	M	J	J	A	S	O	N	D
1												
2												
3												
4												
5												
6												
7												
8												
9												
10												
11												
12												
13												
14												
15												
16												
17												
18												
19												
20												
21												
22												
23												
24												
25												
26												
27												
28												
29												
30												
31												

- [ ] AMAZING
- [ ] HAPPY
- [ ] NORMAL
- [ ] EXCITED
- [ ] STRESSED
- [ ] FOCUSED
- [ ] TIRED / EXHAUSTED
- [ ] DEPRESSED / SAD
- [ ] SICK
- [ ] LOW ENERGY
- [ ] NERVOUS/ ANXIOUS
- [ ] ANGRY
- [ ]
- [ ]

Assign color to a specific mood
and color the squares according to
your mood

Mood Tracker

J F M A M J J A S O N D

1
2
3
4
5
6
7
8
9
10
11
12
13
14
15
16
17
18
19
20
21
22
23
24
25
26
27
28
29
30
31

AMAZING

HAPPY

NORMAL

EXCITED

STRESSED

FOCUSED

TIRED / EXHAUSTED

DEPRESSED / SAD

SICK

LOW ENERGY

NERVOUS/ ANXIOUS

ANGRY

Assign color to a specific mood
and color the squares according to
your mood

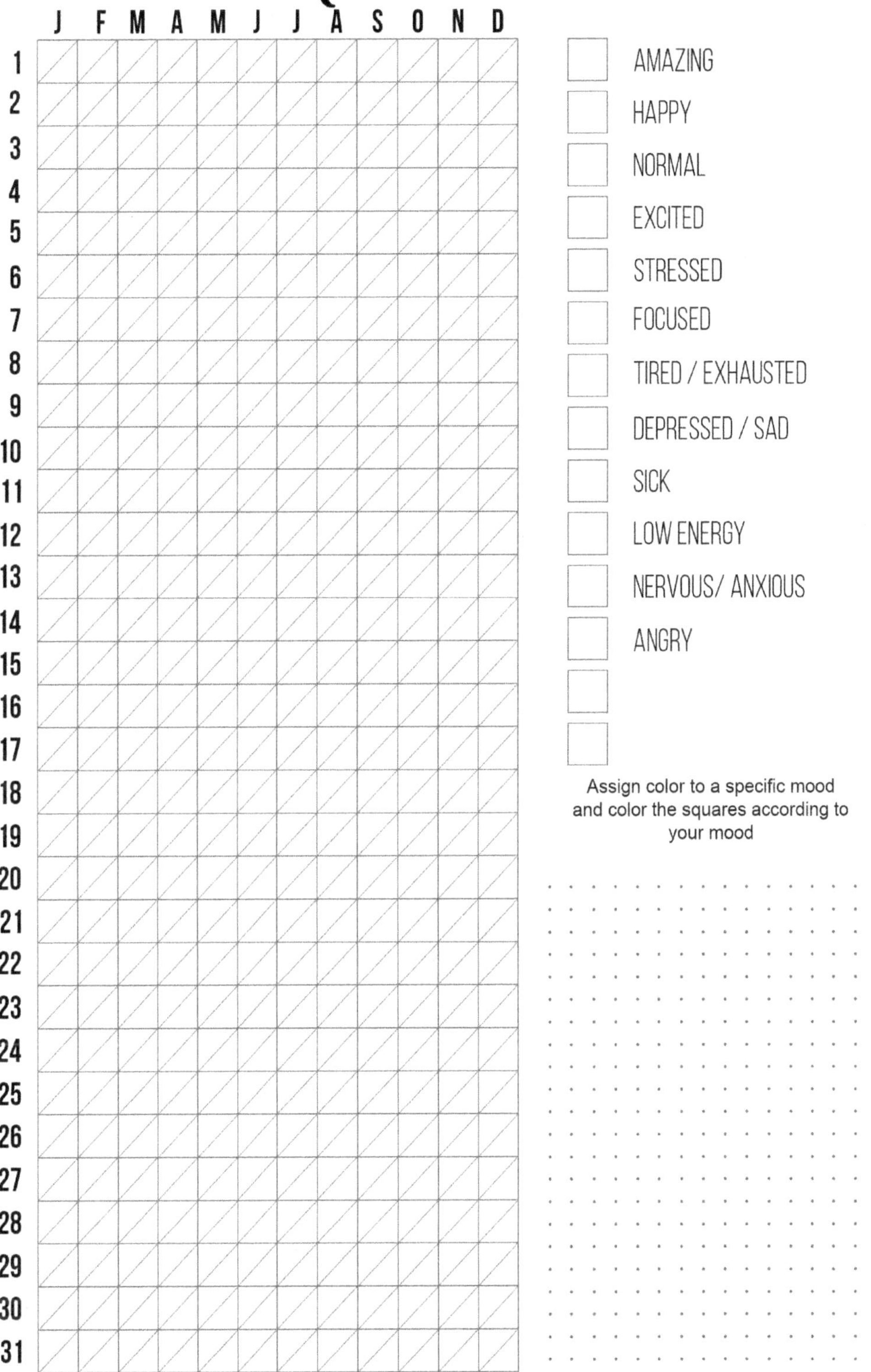

Mood Tracker
J F M A M J J A S O N D
1
2
3
4
5
6
7
8
9
10
11
12
13
14
15
16
17
18
19
20
21
22
23
24
25
26
27
28
29
30
31
AMAZING
HAPPY
NORMAL
EXCITED
STRESSED
FOCUSED
TIRED / EXHAUSTED
DEPRESSED / SAD
SICK
LOW ENERGY
NERVOUS/ ANXIOUS
ANGRY
Assign color to a specific mood
and color the squares according to
your mood

Mood Tracker

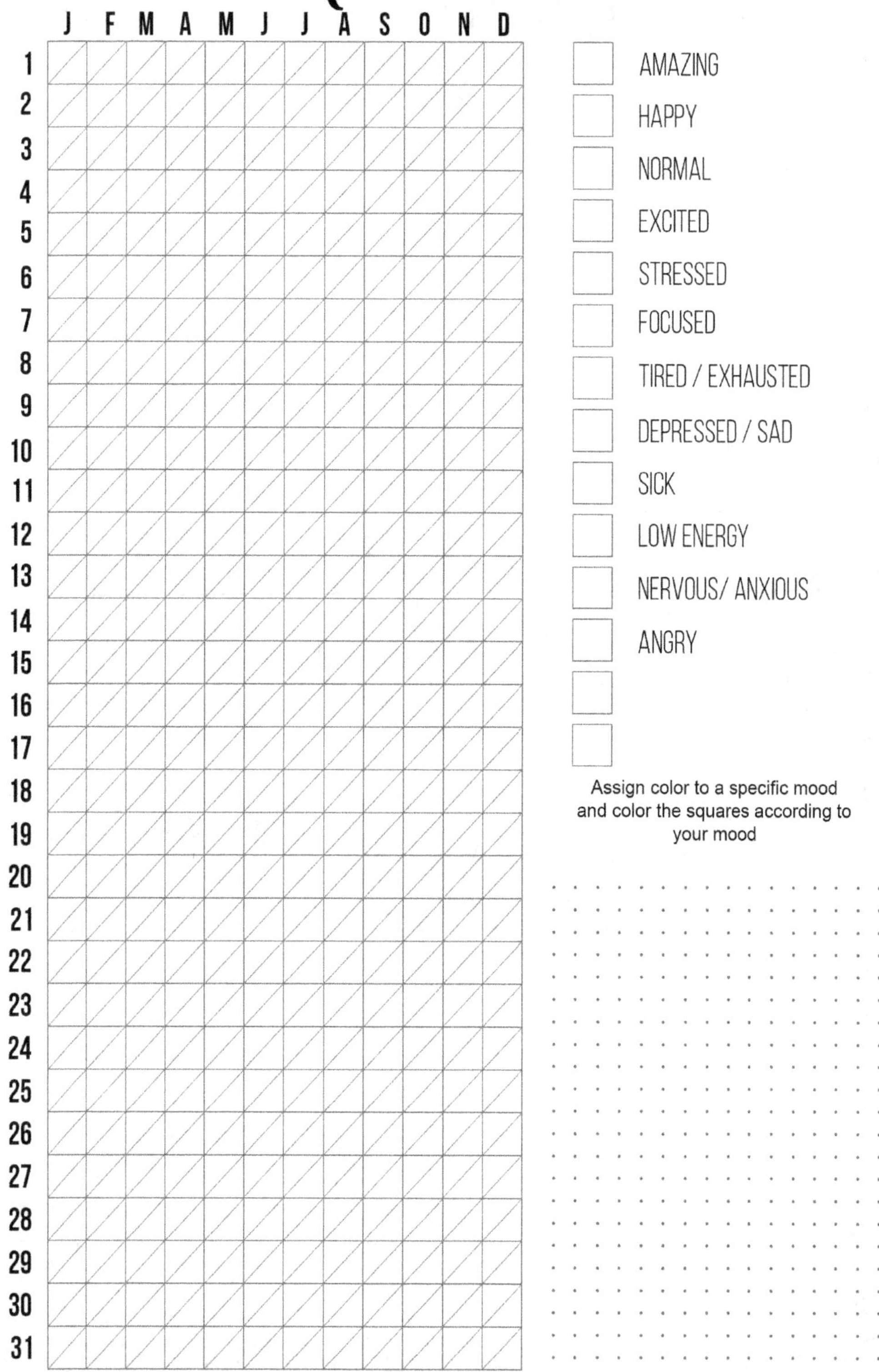

Assign color to a specific mood
and color the squares according to
your mood

AMAZING

HAPPY

NORMAL

EXCITED

STRESSED

FOCUSED

TIRED / EXHAUSTED

DEPRESSED / SAD

SICK

LOW ENERGY

NERVOUS/ ANXIOUS

ANGRY

Mood Tracker

J F M A M J J A S O N D

1 2 3 4 5 6 7 8 9 10 11 12 13 14 15 16 17 18 19 20 21 22 23 24 25 26 27 28 29 30 31

- AMAZING
- HAPPY
- NORMAL
- EXCITED
- STRESSED
- FOCUSED
- TIRED / EXHAUSTED
- DEPRESSED / SAD
- SICK
- LOW ENERGY
- NERVOUS/ ANXIOUS
- ANGRY

Assign color to a specific mood
and color the squares according to
your mood

Mood Tracker

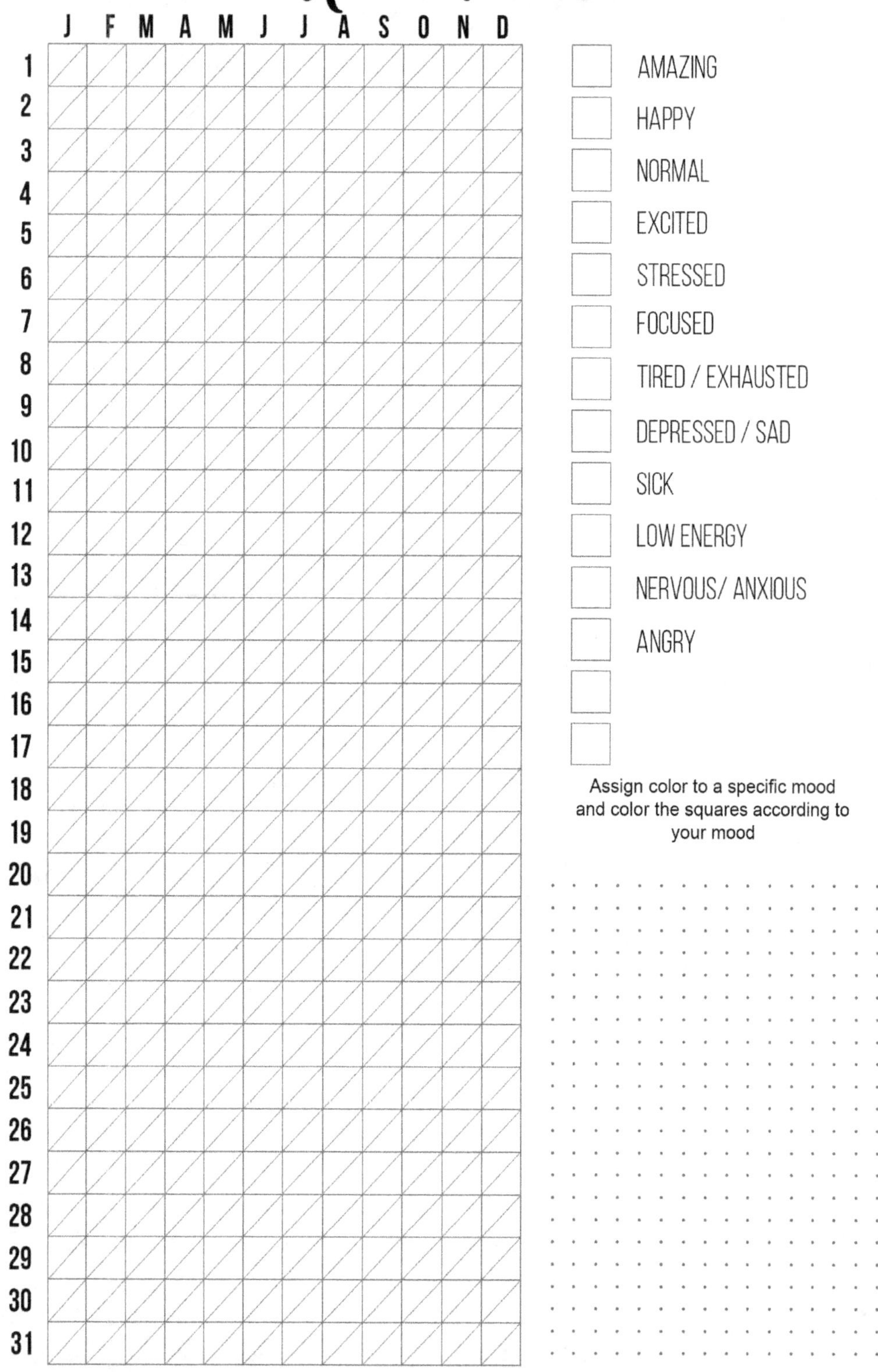

Mood Tracker

J F M A M J J A S O N D

☐	AMAZING
☐	HAPPY
☐	NORMAL
☐	EXCITED
☐	STRESSED
☐	FOCUSED
☐	TIRED / EXHAUSTED
☐	DEPRESSED / SAD
☐	SICK
☐	LOW ENERGY
☐	NERVOUS/ ANXIOUS
☐	ANGRY
☐	
☐	

Assign color to a specific mood
and color the squares according to
your mood

Mood Tracker

J F M A M J J A S O N D

| | 1 2 3 4 5 6 7 8 9 10 11 12 13 14 15 16 17 18 19 20 21 22 23 24 25 26 27 28 29 30 31 |

☐ AMAZING

☐ HAPPY

☐ NORMAL

☐ EXCITED

☐ STRESSED

☐ FOCUSED

☐ TIRED / EXHAUSTED

☐ DEPRESSED / SAD

☐ SICK

☐ LOW ENERGY

☐ NERVOUS/ ANXIOUS

☐ ANGRY

☐

☐

Assign color to a specific mood
and color the squares according to
your mood

Mood Tracker

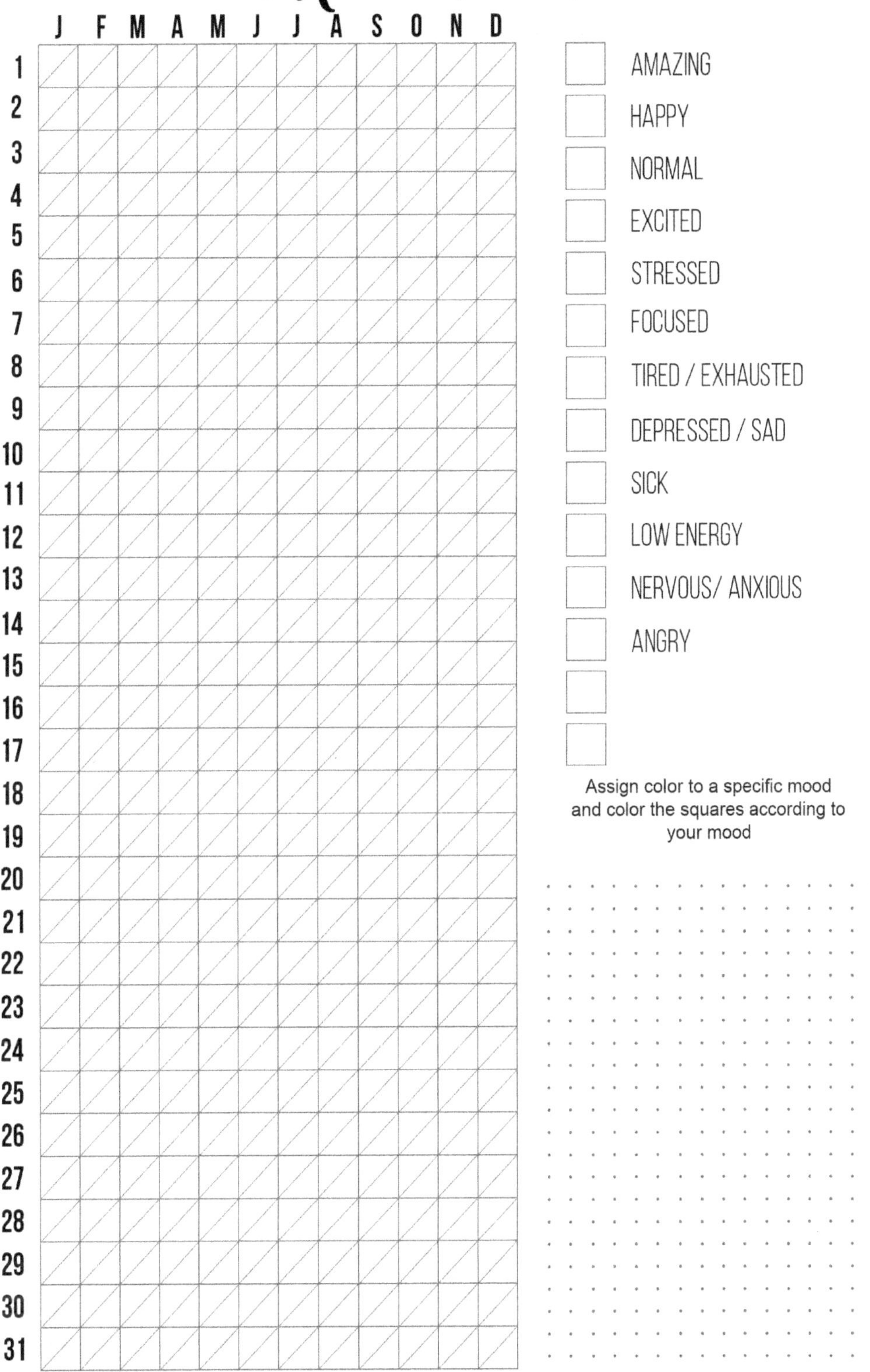

Mood Tracker

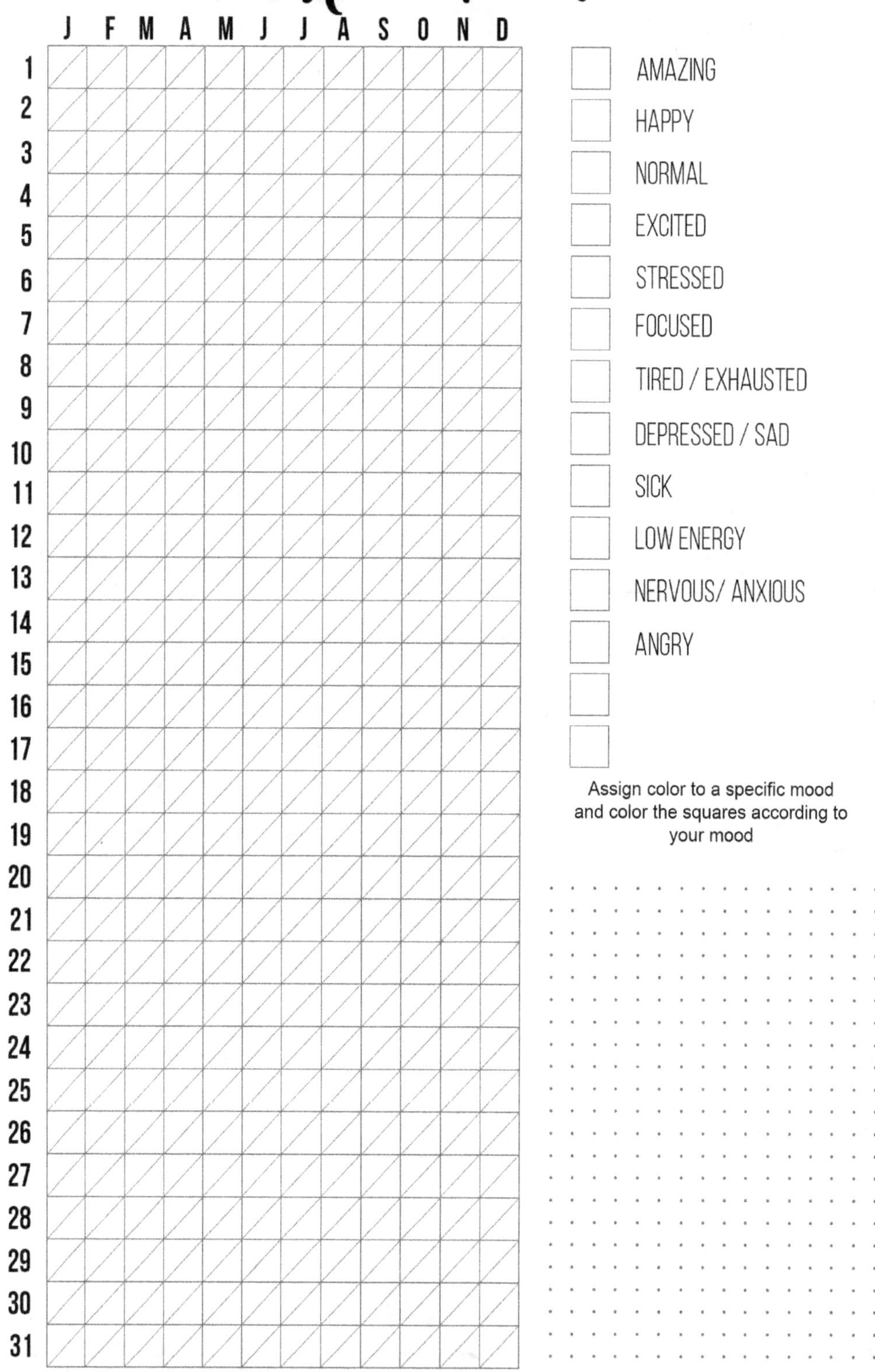

Mood Tracker

J F M A M J J A S O N D

	AMAZING
	HAPPY
	NORMAL
	EXCITED
	STRESSED
	FOCUSED
	TIRED / EXHAUSTED
	DEPRESSED / SAD
	SICK
	LOW ENERGY
	NERVOUS/ ANXIOUS
	ANGRY

Assign color to a specific mood
and color the squares according to
your mood

Mood Tracker

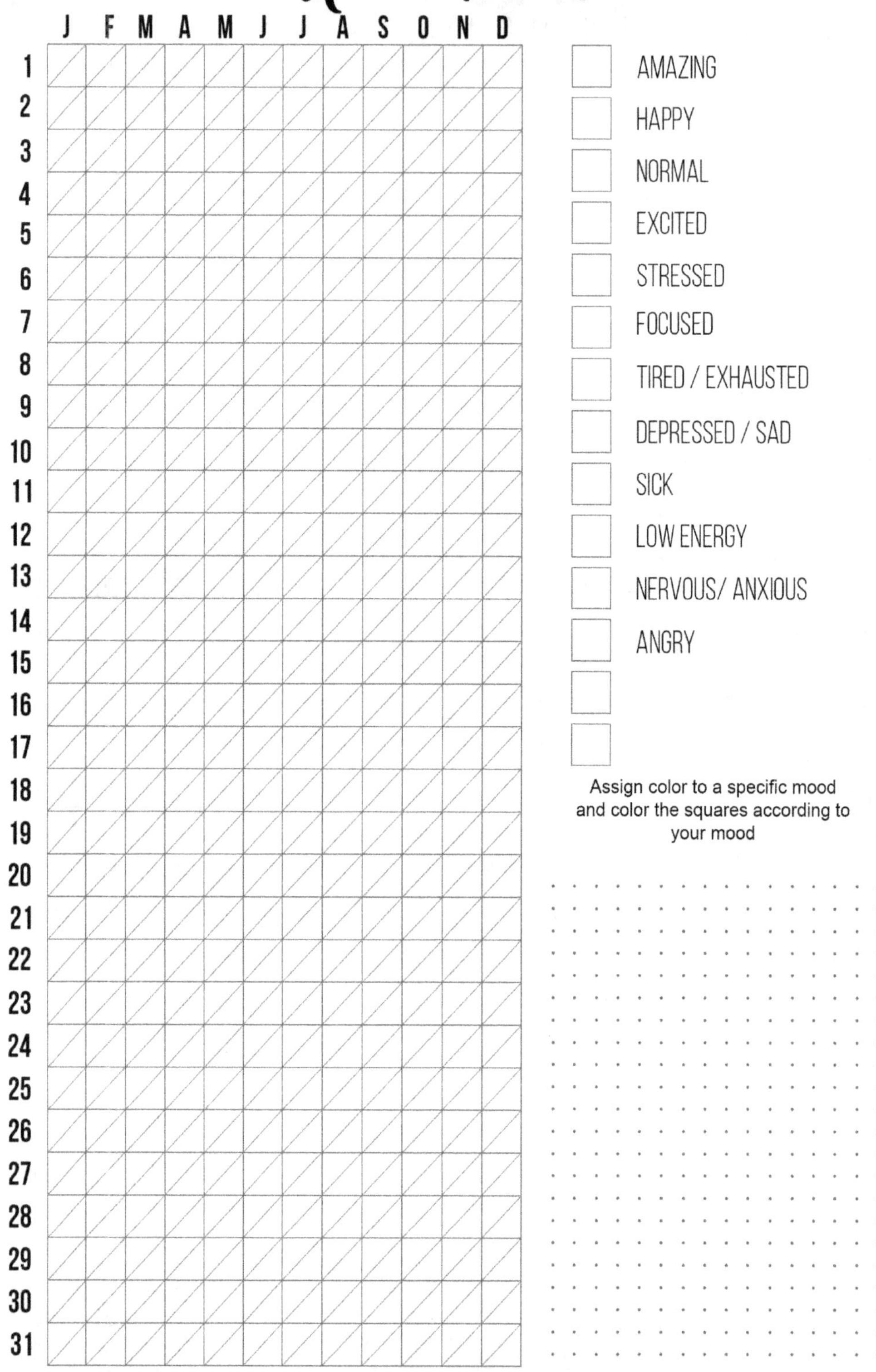

Mood Tracker

J F M A M J J A S O N D

	AMAZING
	HAPPY
	NORMAL
	EXCITED
	STRESSED
	FOCUSED
	TIRED / EXHAUSTED
	DEPRESSED / SAD
	SICK
	LOW ENERGY
	NERVOUS/ ANXIOUS
	ANGRY

Assign color to a specific mood and color the squares according to your mood

Mood Tracker

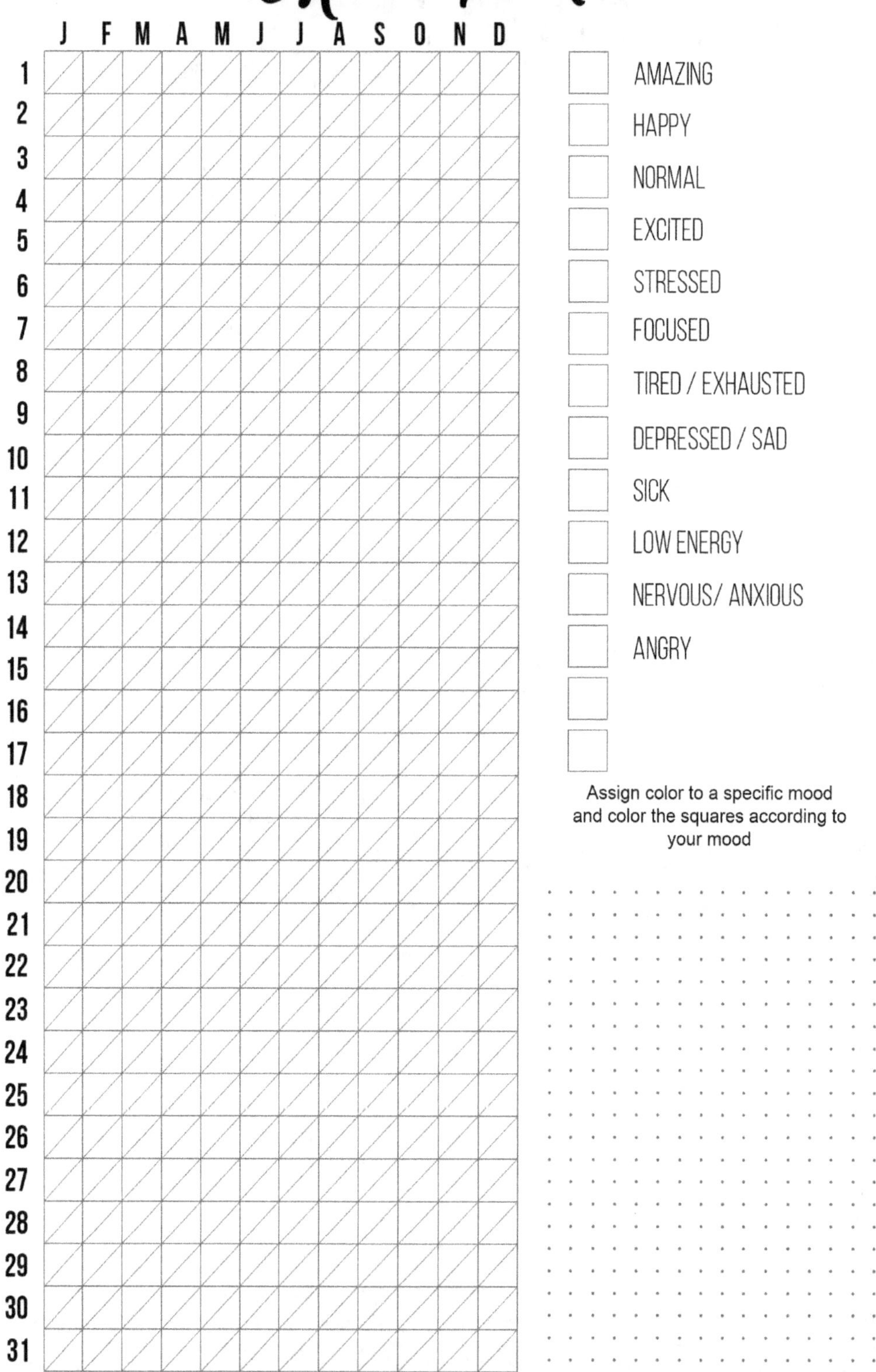

Mood Tracker

J F M A M J J A S O N D

	AMAZING
	HAPPY
	NORMAL
	EXCITED
	STRESSED
	FOCUSED
	TIRED / EXHAUSTED
	DEPRESSED / SAD
	SICK
	LOW ENERGY
	NERVOUS/ ANXIOUS
	ANGRY

Assign color to a specific mood and color the squares according to your mood

Mood Tracker

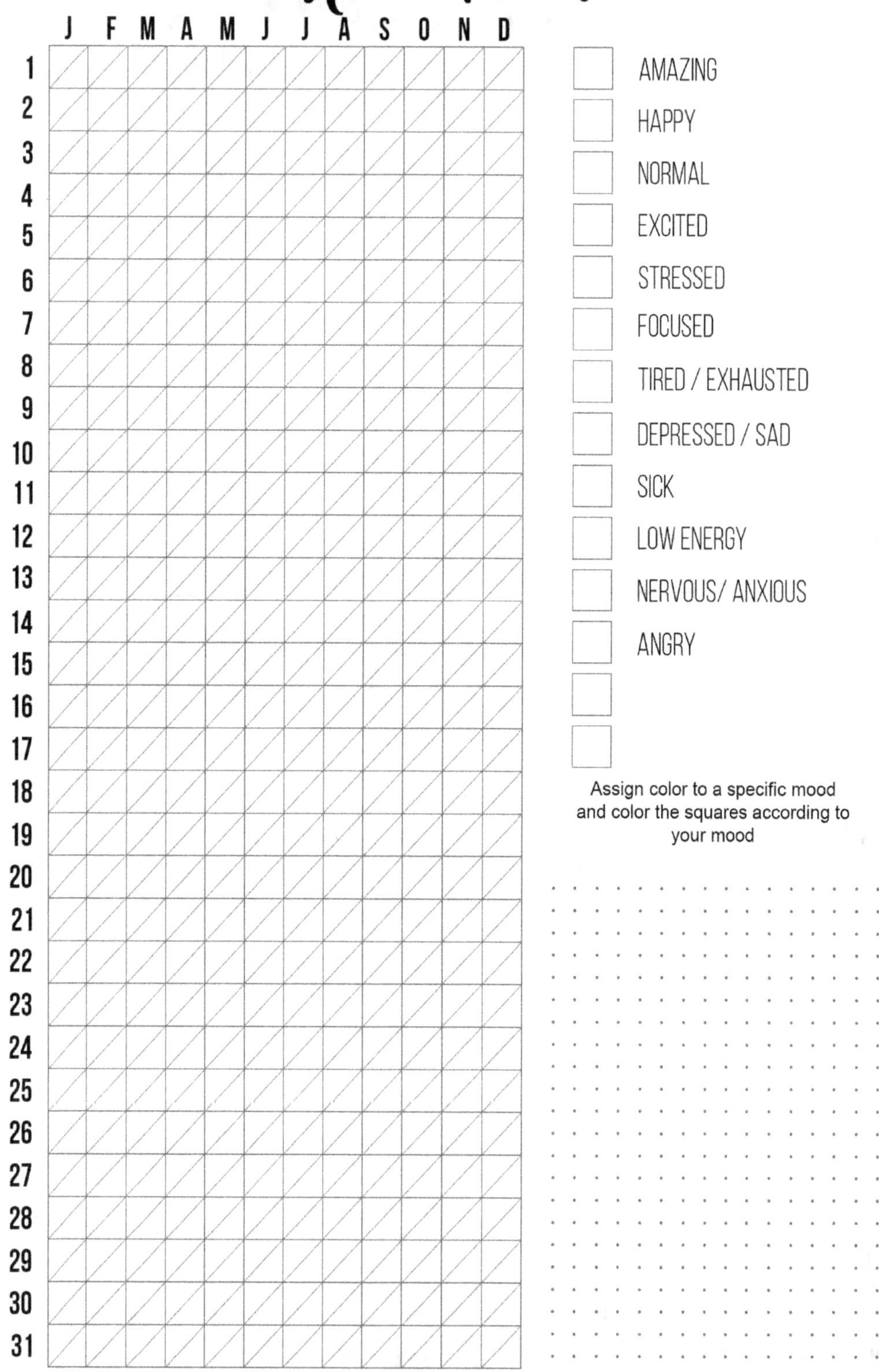

Mood Tracker

J F M A M J J A S O N D

1
2
3
4
5
6
7
8
9
10
11
12
13
14
15
16
17
18
19
20
21
22
23
24
25
26
27
28
29
30
31

AMAZING

HAPPY

NORMAL

EXCITED

STRESSED

FOCUSED

TIRED / EXHAUSTED

DEPRESSED / SAD

SICK

LOW ENERGY

NERVOUS/ ANXIOUS

ANGRY

Assign color to a specific mood
and color the squares according to
your mood

Mood Tracker

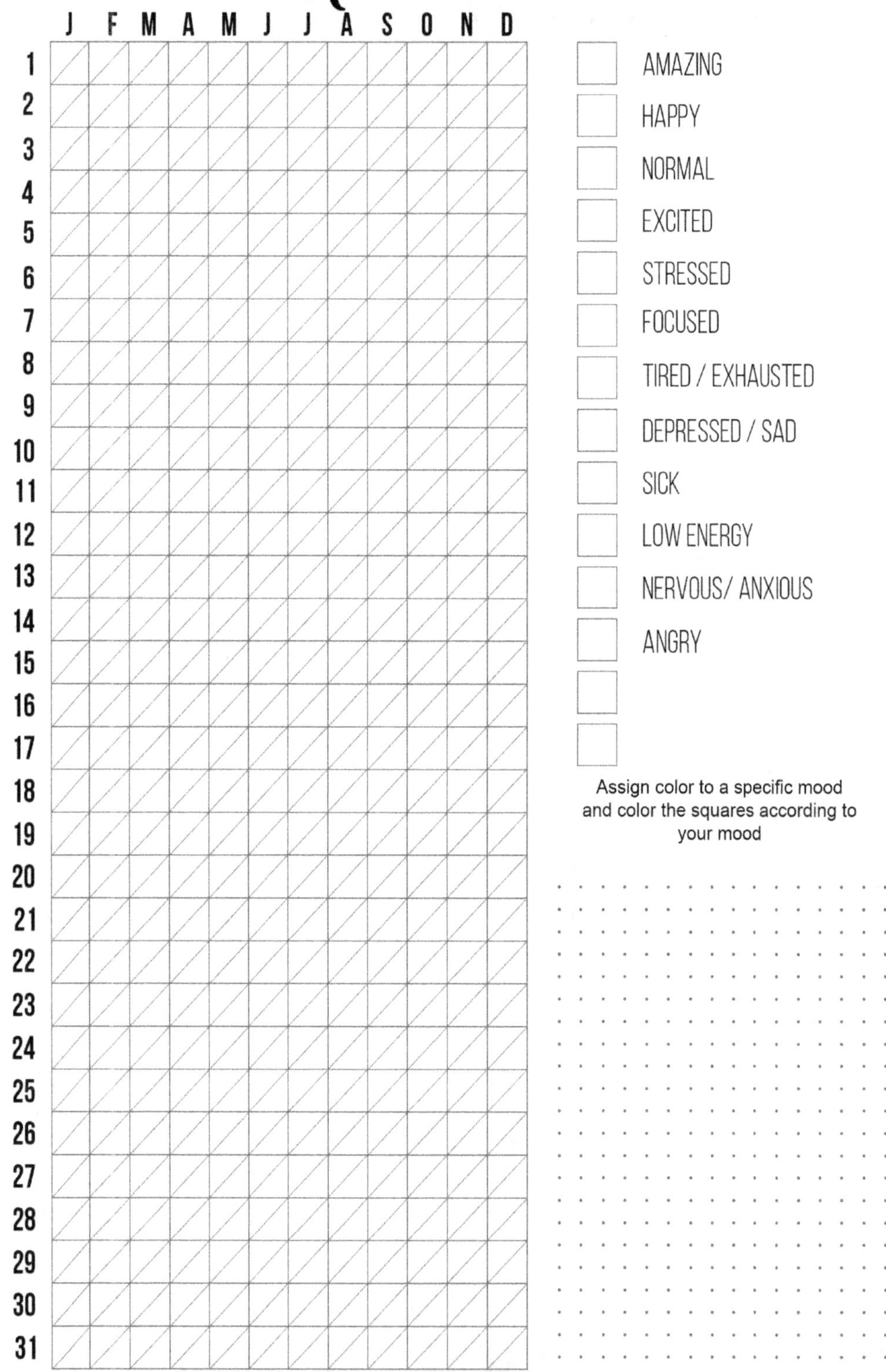

Mood Tracker

J F M A M J J A S O N D

1
2
3
4
5
6
7
8
9
10
11
12
13
14
15
16
17
18
19
20
21
22
23
24
25
26
27
28
29
30
31

- AMAZING
- HAPPY
- NORMAL
- EXCITED
- STRESSED
- FOCUSED
- TIRED / EXHAUSTED
- DEPRESSED / SAD
- SICK
- LOW ENERGY
- NERVOUS/ ANXIOUS
- ANGRY

Assign color to a specific mood
and color the squares according to
your mood

Mood Tracker

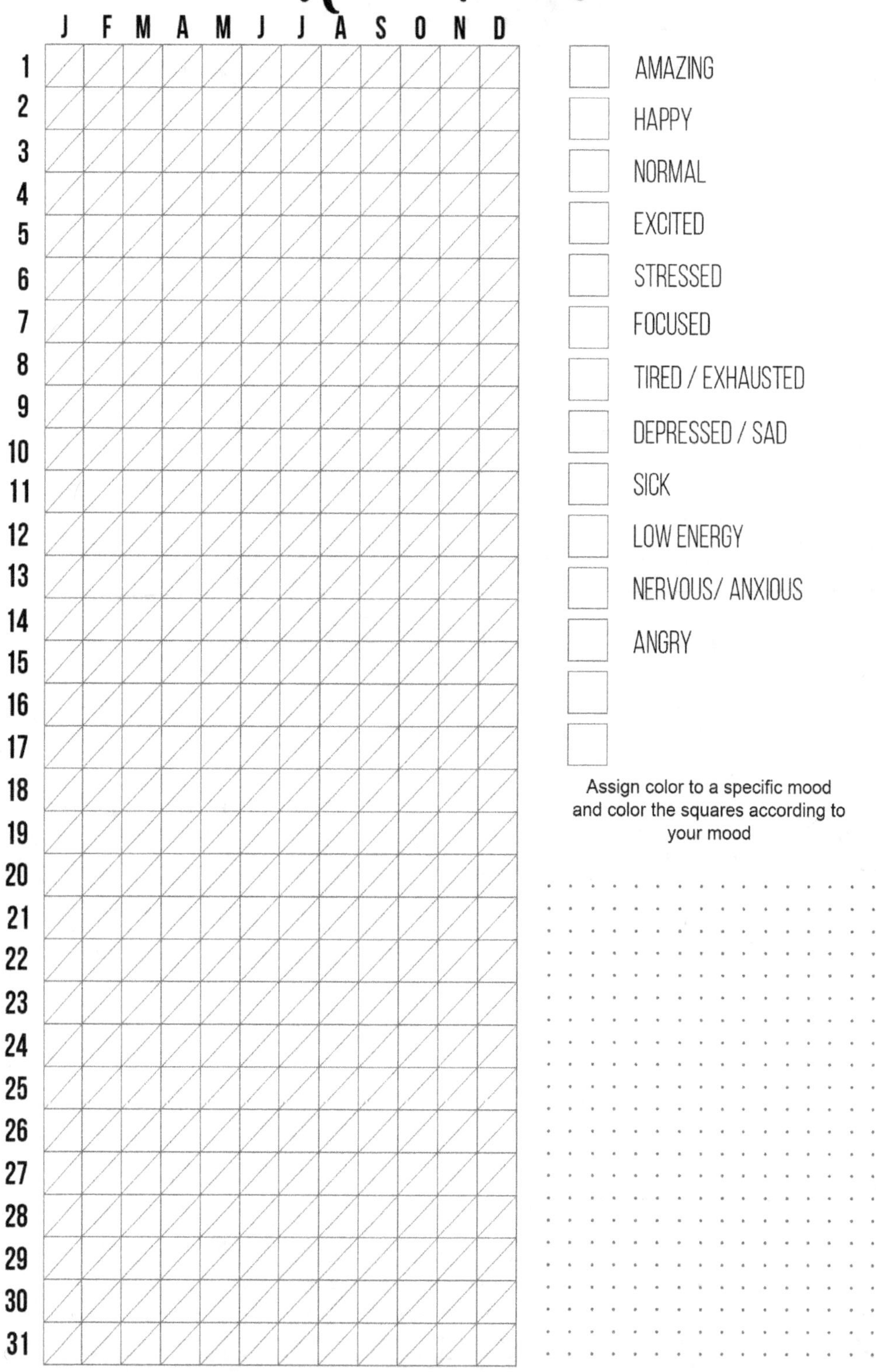

Mood Tracker

AMAZING

HAPPY

NORMAL

EXCITED

STRESSED

FOCUSED

TIRED / EXHAUSTED

DEPRESSED / SAD

SICK

LOW ENERGY

NERVOUS/ ANXIOUS

ANGRY

Assign color to a specific mood
and color the squares according to
your mood

Mood Tracker

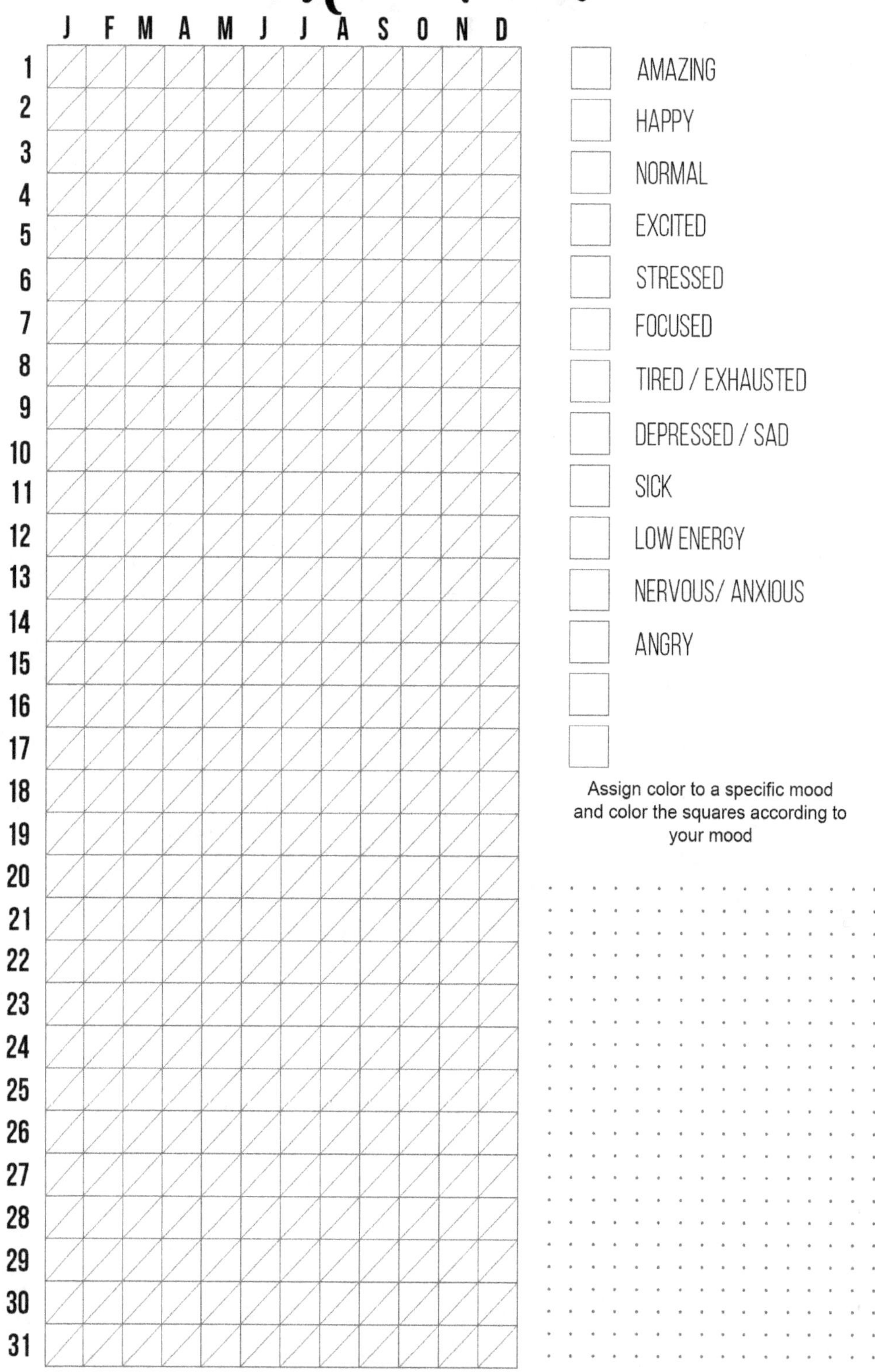